THE FUTURE ECONOMY

A Blueprint for Global Transformation

Jeff Campbell

TABLE OF CONTENTS

ACKNOWLEDGEMENT

This book is dedicated to everyone fighting the struggle. I want to thank the editing team for their tremendous contributions, which were essential in making this book a reality. Their knowledge and assistance have been genuinely outstanding throughout the process. Without their unshakable determination, it might not have been feasible to start our trip.

I want to express my sincere gratitude to my friends and family for supporting me as I entered the world of book publishing and for sticking with me during the difficult times. My professors at Providence School in McLennan and St. Andrew's School in High Prairie deserve a special thank you for giving this book its fundamental components and solid basis.

DEDICATION

Dedicated to everyone fighting the struggle. From High Prairie, Alberta, Canada

PREFACE

World peace is within reach. Advances in technology are opening possibilities to make important systemic changes. Utilizing computer technology for data analysis helps businesses and governments make better decisions. Minimizing financial loss is important for optimizing efficiency. Managing financial constraints has a direct impact on the social issues that every country is facing. A collective and unified effort would be more effective at delivering real solutions. A new global financial system can be created. One that eliminates crime and poverty. It is possible to bring everyone above the poverty line. Every child matters, and everyone should have food and shelter. If you eliminate poverty, you eliminate a lot of the root causes of crime. The emerging markets represent 1000x gains. With development of stock markets and improvements in financial reporting, the upside for growth is tremendous. Job creation and business creation would inject some positivity into the markets. Streamlining operations to improve the people, process, and product of businesses and governments can move the world in a steady and successful direction. A properly functioning global economy would have universal free trade. No tariffs imposed on any goods from any country. A new global financial system that includes all 195 countries would see a free flow of capital and goods between countries never seen before. A new era of cooperation and unity

ABOUT THE AUTHOR

Born in June 1983. A Gemini that see's a future where the world comes together to find solutions and strive for common goals. Grew up in McLennan, Alberta, Canada. A small town with a population of about 1000. Went to school in McLennan at Providence School for grades 1-9. The time at Providence was my most formative years. When you look back you can see how important school teachers are in the development of people. High school was completed at St. Andrew's in High Prairie. My final year of playing hockey was for the Midget "A" Legionnaires. Today the High Prairie Red Wings are the highest level of hockey in my home area. They're games can be watched live on YouTube. Cheering them on as they chase a national championship. And cheering on the Calgary Flames to win a Stanley Cup, my favorite team since childhood. In the 20 years after high school, I mostly worked in the oilfield in Northern Alberta. Lots of days working outdoors in the winter time in colder than -30 degrees celsius. My first child was born in 2006. Her music career will be starting next summer. Second child was born in 2011. Third child born in 2013. The youngest underwent a liver transplant at 9 months of age. The Stollery Children's Hospital in Edmonton, Alberta, will always have a special place in our heart. As well as the David Foster Foundation, they helped us financially during that time. The Public Healthcare system in Canada is amazing. It is a system that should be implemented in every country. High quality care and standards, and free of cost to the patients. Even though I have bias on the matter, I see Alberta as having the best legal framework of any jurisdiction in the world. My current interest is doing courses at the University of Saskatchewan. Pursuing an undergraduate degree and then fulfilling my longtime desire of a Law degree.

INTRODUCTION

World peace is within reach. We are entering a new era of cooperation and unity. Everyone working together to achieve common goals and prosperity. A world without crime and poverty. A world where everyone has food and shelter. It is possible because of advances in technology. People and ideas are being connected, creating a true global collective. A new global financial system that includes all 195 countries can be created. This would enable a free flow of goods and capital in ways the world has never seen before. Job creation and business creation would increase, improving economies and markets worldwide. The emerging markets would see 1000x gains. It is possible to remove the financial constraints that are making it difficult for governments to improve social issues. Give everyone a cell phone and internet connection. The inclusion of every person and they're ideas would create a strong collective. The inclusion of women and advancing women's rights globally is important in a modern and advanced society. A strengthening of traditional family values. Raising people who believe in discipline and living good lives. People who believe that we are better off working together. It is possible to bring everyone above the poverty line. Make improvements to education systems that unlock the STEM (science, technology, engineering, mathematics) ability of the population. The careers and lives of future generations will be ultra high-tech. An integrated peace movement is developing. Moderates from every country in the world are connecting. Resolution to the problems that have lingered internationally will be discovered. Improvements to the processes of how governments communicate can be made. Accepting feedback wether it is good or bad, and respecting differences of opinion. The level of positive energy in the world can be increased. A focused effort to get every single person in the world to have a bank account and a solid financial situation. An increase in financial literacy, so individuals know how to avoid pitfalls and achieve financial goals. A renewed focus on agriculture. Increasing the volume of crop production and crop yield, while decreasing the cost of production is necessary to achieving zero hunger worldwide. An increase in the effort to improve soil health and regeneration, to make life better for future generations.

CHAPTER 1: NEW GLOBAL FINANCIAL SYSTEM THAT INCLUDES ALL 195 COUNTRIES

In a report published ~~during the year~~in 2019, more than sixty international organizations, including the International Monetary Fund, the World Bank Group, and the World Trade Organization, collectively sounded the alarm, warning that unless national and international financial systems are revamped, governments around the world will not keep their commitments on important issues like combating climate change and eliminating poverty by 2030.

The Inter-agency Task Force on Financing for Development, which was made up of more than sixty United Nations Agencies and international organizations, produced the report jointly. The Task Force is substantively edited and coordinated by the UN Department of Economic and Social Affairs' Financing for Sustainable Development Office, which works closely with the World Bank Group, the IMF, the WTO, UNCTAD, and UNDP. The Addis Ababa Action Agenda established the Task Force, which was presided over by Mr. Zhenmin LIU, Under-Secretary-General for Economic and Social Affairs.

The international organizations reported some encouraging findings in their 2019 Financing for Sustainable Development Report. The findings highlighted that investment has grown stronger in some countries, and interest in sustainable investing is rising, with 75% of individual investors expressing interest in how their investments affect the world.

However, investment is declining in many nations, greenhouse gas emissions increased by 1.3% in 2017, and thirty developing nations are now in great danger of or already in debt difficulty. At the same time, it is predicted that global growth will reach a peak of 3%. According to the research, altering the course of financing sustainable development requires more than merely attracting new capital. A supportive financial system, as well as favorable national and international policy frameworks, are necessary for achieving global goals.

The research stressed that it is getting harder to foster favorable conditions. Our economies and communities are rapidly changing because of changes in geopolitics, technology, and the climate, and the current national and global institutions—which had previously assisted in bringing billions out of poverty—are now finding it difficult to adapt because the multilateral system has not produced returns equally for the majority of people living in countries with rising inequality.

According to António Guterres, Secretary-General of the United Nations, "*Trust in the multilateral system itself is eroding, in part because we are not delivering inclusive and sustainable growth for all.*" Making the global trading and financial systems fit for the purpose of advancing sustainable development and encouraging equitable globalization is our shared challenge.

The international agencies suggested taking specific actions to modernize the global institutional framework and increase the sustainability of the world economy and financial system, such as:

- Promoting a shift toward long-term investment horizons with sustainability risks at the center of investment decisions.
- Reviewing mechanisms for restructuring sovereign debt to address more complex debt instruments and a more diverse landscape of creditors.
- Updating the multilateral trading system.
- Addressing issues with tax systems that prevent nations from raising enough money in an increasingly digitalized global economy.
- Addressing growing cross-border market concentration that has an impact on inequality.

The paper offers a road map for nations to restructure their public and private financial systems to raise money for sustainable investment at the national level. It presents tools to help nations match their national sustainable development aims and strategies with their financial policies. The report discusses opportunities and challenges in new technologies and fintech in one instance. The appeal of fintech is obvious, given that more than half a billion people now have access to financial services in recent years. Regulators, however, find it difficult to keep up as new players enter and quickly alter the financing market. Fintech is becoming more and more important, and if unchecked, activities outside of the regulatory framework could threaten financial stability.

With regulatory measures that address these issues, fintech's potential may be realized, but they must be put in place without impeding innovation. To achieve this, the paper stresses the significance of conversations among fintech firms, financial institutions, and regulators. It concludes that rather than by institutional type, the regulatory focus will need to shift to financial activities and their underlying hazards, regardless of the company that engages in them.

According to Mr. Liu Zhenmin, the Task Force's Chair and Under-Secretary-General for Economic and Social Affairs, *"We have a significant potential to resolve obstacles in sustainable funding in 2019."* Governments have a duty to reaffirm their commitment to multilateralism and to implement public policies that will ensure a sustainable and prosperous future.

The Need for a Global Financial System

The COVID-19 epidemic and the havoc it has caused on the global economy have brought to light the need for a stronger global financial safety net that offers more security for underdeveloped and emerging market economies (EMDEs). These nations have limited room for maneuvering when faced with such major global shocks because they already experience considerable economic pressures. Even the advanced economies should be interested in improving these nations' ability to resist such shocks, given their growing significance in the global economy.

EMDEs experienced an abrupt halt in capital inflows and downward pressure on their exchange rates at the start of the epidemic. In stark contrast to the decrease in government bond yields in advanced economies, funding conditions tightened even for those nations with relatively good macroeconomic fundamentals. Due to the current low-interest rate around the world and the depreciating value of the dollar, many EMDEs, especially larger nations, are again experiencing a resurgent inflow of capital. Even though this offers short-term comfort, these countries' macroeconomic management is made more difficult by these cycles of capital flow pauses and surges.

Because major advanced economies depend on monetary policy measures, both conventional and unconventional, for economic support and because these policies have whiplash effects, EMDEs will continue to be susceptible to capital movement and exchange rate volatility. Many EMDEs continue to be vulnerable due to their reliance on dollar funding, and as a result, the Fed's decisions and the dollar's trajectory, in particular, have a significant impact on them.

When they needed access to the international financial markets to combat the pandemic and support their economy, a number of EMDEs with significant levels of external debt and balance of payments vulnerabilities saw sovereign debt downgrades. Countries with low incomes confront much more difficulties. Their export markets and economies have collapsed, leaving many of them struggling to repay crushing debt loads. Many low-income countries have high levels of sovereign debt, and the pandemic is likely to make matters worse because there are not many other domestic or international revenue sources available in these nations.

The global financial architecture needed to be updated even before COVID-19 to keep up with the changing dynamics of the world economy, but the pandemic has revealed the full extent of these flaws, highlighting the urgency of reform. To make the global financial system more useful in the post-COVID world, the international community will need to take some risky measures.

A mechanism to steadily increase the International Monetary Fund's (IMF) lending capacity to a level commensurate with the growth in the financial system's complexity and the size of the global economy should be included in the post-COVID-19 global financial system. The IMF is the most crucial organization in the international financial system for providing safety nets to nations experiencing financial crises, but due to resource constraints, it has been unable to meet the unprecedented number of requests for assistance.

The institution's total resources are only close to $1 trillion, or 1.1 percent of the world's GDP. While this sum might be adequate to finance a few country crises, it is insufficient to handle systemic crises like COVID-19, and as the global GDP rises, this resource's share of GDP will decrease. The excessive reliance on non-quota resources for funding, such as the New Arrangements to Borrow (NAB) and bilateral borrowing agreements, which are temporary and at the discretion of donor countries, poses a further risk to the IMF's resources and is a significant source of uncertainty for potential borrowers. The IMF's resources will drop to about $450 billion if these facilities are not extended before they expire, which is scheduled to happen soon.

Another instrument in the global financial system's toolbox, the IMF's power to issue fresh Special Drawing Rights (SDRs), should be consistently used as needed to supplement the already available credit facilities. Only four times in its history has the IMF used this mechanism, the last occasion being in response to a G-20 request during the 2008–2009 global financial crisis (GFC). A supermajority of 85% is necessary to activate it, which is a lot more than the combined voting share of all EMDEs. The lack of the required super-majority support caused a proposal to issue new SDRs as the pandemic spread throughout the world.

SDRs that have already been generated but have not yet been utilized by the beneficiary countries may also exist. If the pool of underutilized SDRs is large enough, it would also be beneficial to reallocate funds from richer nations with access to alternative funding sources to less developed nations. The existing SDR reallocation is largely voluntary, which restricts the IMF's ability to effectively utilize this tool. As a result, the allocation of SDRs is entirely subject to the will of the holders of allocated and unused SDRs or, in the case of new SDRs, the majority shareholders. An improvement would be a system that allows the IMF to reallocate SDRs to areas where they are most needed.

Establishing a framework to systematically broaden access to short-term foreign exchange liquidity in numerous nations would be the third reform. The majority of EMDEs do not have access to the bilateral swap arrangements, which have evolved into a common tool among central banks of advanced economies during global shocks since the GFC. The swap lines provided by the Federal Reserve have assisted in supplying dollar liquidity to international financial markets during the COVID-19 pandemic. Even so, the majority of these swap lines are with the central banks of other developed nations.

The Fed did provide dollar funding lines to more nations during the height of the pandemic, with the lines being secured by the central banks' holdings of US Treasury securities. But, such impromptu solutions fall short of a more organized strategy. In addition to being more efficient, institutionalized emergency liquidity assistance mechanisms would also lessen the incentive for EMDEs to engage in self-insurance through reserve accumulation, which is ineffective on both the national and international levels.

The G-20 announced a debt standstill initiative (DSSI), calling on all creditors to grant delays in debt repayment for the least developed countries through the end of 2020 in the absence of a sufficiently robust global safety net. It is anticipated that the DSSI will raise $12 billion for the qualified nations. The result has been far short of expectations so far, coming in at only $4 billion. The legitimate worries of eligible countries that participation might result in a sovereign downgrade and undo strenuous efforts to gain access to international capital markets are among the main barriers.

The financial system currently lacks a working mechanism for an orderly restructuring of the external debt of EMDEs. To help manage the predicted rise in the number of nations in debt crisis over the next few years, establishing one should be a top priority. Due to the significantly altered economic environment and creditor landscape, restructuring debt for a larger number of countries will be challenging, especially when multiple private creditors are involved. There is still a sizable stock of sovereign bonds without collective action clauses (CACs), despite the fact that the clauses were improved in 2014 and were useful in some sovereign debt restructurings. The time may be right to take into account additional innovative solutions, such as well-capitalized and creditworthy Special Purpose Vehicles, possibly financed by SDRs, to aid in the restructuring of private sector debt.

CHAPTER 2: GLOBAL FREE TRADE — NO TARIFFS

Trade is essential in order to eradicate poverty worldwide. Open economies tend to develop more quickly, innovate, increase productivity, and give their citizens more chances and higher incomes. By providing consumers with more cheap goods and services, open trade also benefits households with lower incomes. Economic growth and poverty reduction are aided locally and worldwide by integrating with the global economy through trade and global value chains. The WBG has facilitated cross-border trade, improved the dependability of logistical services, and streamlined the customs clearance process in nations like Bosnia and Herzegovina, Macedonia, and Indonesia. These initiatives, along with others, contribute to the development of a more open, dependable, and predictable global trading system.

The expansion of the world economy was largely due to international trade. Global events have an impact on supply and demand, and consequently prices, in the global economy. A rise in labor costs, for instance, could be brought on by a political change in Asia. A Malaysian-based American shoe firm may see an increase in production expenses as a result of this, which would raise the cost of a pair of sneakers that an American customer may buy at their neighborhood mall.

Wealthy nations can employ their resources—such as labor, technology, or capital—more effectively thanks to global commerce. Different nations are blessed with various natural resources and assets, including land, labor, capital, and technology. This enables some nations to manufacture the same commodity more rapidly and cheaply or more effectively. They might sell it for less than other nations. If a nation cannot effectively manufacture a good, it can nonetheless receive it through trade with another nation.

Through commerce, nations can access commodities and services that might not be accessible domestically and grow their markets. Market competition has increased as a result of global trade. This ultimately leads to more competitive pricing, which lowers the cost of the final product for the consumer. Trade and globalization open new opportunities, but they also come with difficulties. For a variety of reasons, developing nations may find it difficult to compete on a global level. Some of them are stated ~~down~~ below:

- Weak or ineffective logistics, customs, or transportation systems.
- A lack of connectedness in the financial markets, information technology, or telecommunications.
- Complex regulatory frameworks that deter fresh investment.
- Big market players or cartels engage in anticompetitive activity that stunts innovation, productivity, or market expansion.

The world's poor, who are frequently disproportionately cut off from global, regional, or even local markets, are seriously impacted by the growing complexity of commerce. Poorly connected to vibrant economic centers, poverty is frequently concentrated in geographic regions. They are less able to diversify their products and skills, are not integrated into global production chains, and miss out on possibilities to create trained competitive workforces. Increasing commerce has distributional repercussions as well. Even though more trade generally benefits economies greatly, as competition heats up and a large number of high-quality employments are created in export-oriented industries, the pay of workers in import-oriented industries may suffer, or some people may lose their jobs.

The World Bank has initiated several approaches that support an open, predictable, rules-based multilateral trading system with the aim of assisting nations and profiting from such a system. Important tactics on the agenda include:

- Facilitating trade, managing logistics, and managing borders in order to assist nations in joining global value chains (GVCs).
- Trade agreements: providing technical assistance to countries and assisting in the execution of promises made under these accords.
- Trade and competitiveness are prioritized at the heart of national development strategies.
- Aid for Trade: The Bank Group is the main source of *Aid for Trade*, a multilateral effort aimed at helping developing nations, particularly low-income ones, by integrating into the global economy among multilateral institutions.

- Promoting growth and shared prosperity through the opening and transformation of markets.

Trade volume growth in 2017 was 4.3%, which was the fastest in 6 years. Countries whose GDP is expanding, businesses that sell items across borders, and consumers who can get goods and services at lower prices are the driving forces behind higher trade levels. The World Bank collaborates with governments to develop and put into effect policies that maximize competitiveness, boost connectivity, and facilitate trade to further improve global commerce. The World Bank Group assists its client nations in enhancing their market access and global economic involvement in order to achieve the dual goals of reducing extreme poverty and boosting shared prosperity.

The World Bank's Trade Facilitation Support Program (TFSP) and the Umbrella Facility for Trade are just two of the organizations that provide trade advisory and support work that spans 111 Bank lending projects in 57 countries, 219 Bank advisory tasks in 64 countries, and 56 IFC Advisory projects in 35 countries (UF).

The WBG's involvement in trade at the international, regional, and national levels has improved trade competitiveness by fostering predictability in trade operations, reducing a range of trade costs, expanding and establishing new markets, and putting a priority on inclusive trade integration.

Free Trade vs. Protectionism

The ~~easier~~ easiest of the two theories is free trade. Another name for this strategy is *laissez-faire* economics. There are no trade limitations under a laissez-faire system. The fundamental tenet is that efficient manufacturing will be ensured by global supply and demand forces. Nothing needs to be done to safeguard or encourage commerce and growth because market forces will take care of these things on their own. According to protectionism, it's crucial to regulate global commerce to guarantee that markets operate as intended. Supporters of this idea try to direct the market in accordance with their belief that market inefficiencies may impede the advantages of global commerce. Protectionism, tariffs, subsidies, and quotas are the most frequently used ones. These tactics make an effort to address any inefficiency in the global market.

International commerce can increase a nation's capacity to manufacture and acquire commodities by providing the possibility for specialization and, consequently, more effective resource utilization. However, critics of international free trade have claimed that it still permits inefficiencies that put developing countries at risk. The world economy is unquestionably undergoing constant development.

Why Don't We Trade Globally?

Why isn't international trade open between nations? Why do some nations continue to be impoverished while others benefit from free trade? There are numerous causes, but economists believe that rent-seeking is the most significant one. When one group organizes and presses the government to advance its interests, rent-seeking happens.

American shoe manufacturers are aware of the free-trade argument, but they also realize that cheaper foreign shoes will harm their interests. No one in the shoe industry wants to lose their job or see profits fall in the short term, even if doing so would allow workers to be more productive than if they switched from making shoes to making computers. This desire might prompt the shoemakers to advocate for tax benefits specifically for their goods or higher levies (or even outright bans) on imported footwear. There are numerous calls to protect American jobs and traditional American crafts, despite the fact that such protectionist measures would ultimately make American workers and customers less wealthy and less productive.

International commerce not only boosts productivity but also gives nations access to the global economy, promoting the possibility of foreign direct investment (FDI). Theoretically, economies can grow more effectively and readily join the competitive market. Foreign capital and skills can enter the country through FDI for the receiving government. It increases employment rates and, in theory, boosts the gross domestic product (GDP). FDI offers business expansion and growth for the investor, which results in better revenues.

The Comparative Advantage Theory

David Ricardo, an English political economist, is credited with developing the concept of comparative advantage. Although it has been speculated that Ricardo's mentor, James Mill, likely created the concept and snuck it into Ricardo's book on the fly, comparative advantage is covered in Ricardo's book *On the Principles of Political Economy and Taxation*, which was published in 1817.

The concept of comparative advantage demonstrated how Portugal and England both benefited from specialization and trade based on their own comparative advantages. In this instance, Portugal was able to produce wine for a reasonable price, while England was able to produce cloth for a reasonable price. Each nation would finally acknowledge these facts, according to Ricardo, and quit seeking to produce the more expensive commodity.

China's comparative advantage over the US in terms of labor costs ~~serve~~ serves as a more modern illustration of comparative advantage. Simple consumer goods are produced by Chinese employees at a far lower opportunity cost. In specialized, capital-intensive work, the U.S. has a competitive edge. American employees generate high-end products or profitable investment prospects for less money. These types of trade and specialization are advantageous for each nation.

The notion of comparative advantage contributes to the explanation of why protectionism has historically failed. It may result in an immediate local advantage in the form of new jobs if a country withdraws from an international trade agreement or if a government applies tariffs, but this is rarely a long-term solution to a trade problem. That nation will eventually become less competitive than its neighbors, who were already better able to produce these goods at a lower opportunity cost.

The idea of comparative advantage states that any nation would eventually acknowledge these truths and give up trying to produce the more expensive ~~good~~ goods domestically in favor of trading. England would probably stop making wine, and Portugal would probably stop making fabric over time. Both nations would understand that it was in their best interests to trade with one another in order to acquire the other rather than diverting their energies from producing what they were comparably better at locally. England and Portugal came to the realization that by concentrating on the goods for which they had a comparative advantage, they might increase their output. The Portuguese would then start producing wine solely, while the English would exclusively produce cotton.

Each nation can produce a specialized output of 20 units annually and trade an equal amount of both goods. As a result, both products are now available in each nation for less money. The potential cost of producing both items is higher for both countries than the cost of specialization. Absolute advantage can be contrasted with comparative advantage. Only when each producer has an absolute advantage in producing a particular good does absolute advantage result in clear profits from specialization and commerce. A producer would never export anything if they possessed any absolute advantages. However, we do observe that countries with a comparative advantage, even those without an absolute glaring advantage, benefit from trade.

The Bottom Line

The advantages of international trading for a corporation include diversification, a broader pool of prospective customers, which increases earnings and revenues, perhaps less rivalry in a foreign market that hasn't yet been penetrated, and potential gains from fluctuating currency rates. International trade results from regional disparities between each country. International trade is typically sparked by disparities in technology, education, demand, governmental regulations, labor laws, natural resources, wages, and financial opportunities. Government policies that obstruct commerce internationally and safeguard home markets are known as trade barriers. These include import and export permits, tariffs, quotas, subsidies, and standardization.

The globalization of economies has increased their interdependence, and most economies place a significant emphasis on international commerce. It gives customers more options and boosts competition, forcing companies to make things that are both affordable and of great quality, which is good for these customers. By concentrating on producing the items in which they have a competitive advantage, nations also profit from international commerce. International commerce has proved to be beneficial to economies as a whole, even when some nations restrict it through tariffs and quotas in order to protect home industries.

CHAPTER 3: INCREASE THE VALUES OF THE LOWEST NATIONAL CURRENCIES, THE EMERGING MARKETS

Developed markets like the US and Europe are very important to emerging markets. The performance of emerging market economies is significantly impacted by changes in exchange rates relative to the US dollar because a major percentage of their credit, commerce, and debt are priced in dollars. In emerging markets, abrupt fluctuations in exchange rates are usually linked to increasing financial instability, tighter financing conditions, and capital flight. It can be difficult to pinpoint the exact causes of these changes, though, as both domestic and global forces interact to determine the relative strengths of different currencies.

Between January and August of 2018, the currencies of emerging markets experienced a severe drop. Emerging market currencies experienced a severe sell-off during the first eight months of 2018, which was followed by capital outflows and increasing volatility i~~o~~n the financial markets. The composite index of the nominal effective exchange rates of emerging market currencies fell by 3.6% between January and August of that year, while bilateral exchange rates against the US dollar experienced a much larger reaction, falling by more than 20% in certain cases. Unsettling financial market fluctuations in some countries have put financial stability in danger, and they may have an effect on advanced economies as well. Significant currency declines increase borrowing costs for emerging market economies, decreasing the possibility of economic growth.

Exchange rate movements cannot be explained by differences in interest rates alone. Theoretically, fluctuations in interest rates are what cause changes in exchange rates, according to the uncovered interest rate parity hypothesis. This holds that the bilateral exchange rate should move in a manner that is determined by changes in the interest rate differential between the two countries, with the high-yielding currency appreciating in relation to the low-yielding currency. However, in practice, a sizable amount of exchange rate movements cannot be attributed to variations in interest rates but rather to variations in the risk premium.

Several economic variables, such as indicators of investors' risk appetite or market volatility, are connected with the risk premium but are not adequately captured by short-term interest rate differentials. In actuality, variations in interest rates to the US dollar only partially explain changes in the exchange rates of developing countries in 2018.

We gain a better understanding of the factors influencing currency swings by using a model that augments the traditional interest rate regression with assessments of global risk appetite and US characteristics. Beyond interest rates, changes in the degree of global risk appetite and the knock-on effects of US events are the two main determinants affecting the value of emerging market currencies. Because increasing risk-taking among market players frequently results in capital inflows into emerging markets, which improve the value of those markets' currencies, the degree of risk appetite globally influences currencies.

The US dollar's unique position in the world's monetary system is another important consideration. When the US dollar is strong, which happens when the US economy is experiencing rapid economic development and ~~high~~ high-interest rates, capital tends to flow from emerging markets to the US, which weakens the currencies of developing markets. US shocks can enter emerging world economies via this mechanism.

[1]Verdelhan (2018) proposes a simple methodology to examine the relative impact of each of the two forces for movements in emerging market currencies. The standard model in which exchange rate movements are related to interest rate differentials is enhanced by two components. One, which is sometimes referred to as a "dollar factor," seeks to determine how changes in the United States affect the currencies of emerging markets. It is added by including a component in the regression that gauges the typical change in exchange rates between emerging markets and the US currency.

A financial shock that is solely US-based may be expected to have a comparable impact on all bilateral exchange rates for the US dollar~~, t~~. Therefore, looking at changes that are shared by a lot of these exchange rates

---

[1] Verdelhan, A., "The Share of Systemic Variation in Bilateral Exchange Rates", Journal of Finance, Vol. 73, No 1, 2018.

should highlight shocks that are specific to the US currency. The second factor, sometimes known as the "carry factor" in the literature, accounts for risk-driven currency swings in developing markets that are independent ~~to~~ of US shocks. The difference between shifts in the exchange rates of currencies with high yields and those with low yields is how it is defined.

When investors engage in carry trades, which include selling assets in low-yielding currencies to buy assets in high-yielding currencies, they are exposed to global risks through the exchange rate. This is because currencies with ~~high~~ high-interest rates usually experience declines during recessions or periods of low risk-taking. ~~If~~ As a result, as global risk rises, the gap between the two portfolios' exchange rate returns expands, increasing the mechanical relationship between this component and global risk.

When these two factors are included in the base model, the amount of ~~the~~ volatility in emerging market currencies that can be explained rises considerably. National trends make up the remaining component, which is unaccounted for by these foreign or American influences. It may also take into account factors that short-term money market rates do not completely reflect, such as shifts in forecasts for the future course of the domestic economy or market perceptions of the currency.

Two main factors—spillovers from US shocks and global risk, according to the analysis of the period up to August 2018—were responsible for the depreciation of emerging market currencies in relation to the US dollar. This is in line with the tightening of the financial conditions in emerging markets and the rise in US yields that were observed around the same time. In Turkey and Argentina, where domestic political upheaval is believed to have been the main factor influencing currency rate movements, there are notable exceptions. The model also shows that domestic monetary policies, which were meant to increase interest rate gaps with the US, were mostly unable to counteract the effects of US and international factors that were weakening currencies.

The impact of the US dollar factor has decreased after August 2018, indicating that no additional currency spillover impacts to emerging market countries have occurred since that time. However, country-specific factors have a tendency to strengthen emerging market currencies, suggesting that since the turmoil ~~on~~ in the financial markets in the summer of 2018, domestic conditions and development prospects have improved in emerging nations.

Over the past 20 to 30 years, emerging markets have not only undergone rapid expansion but also a dramatic change in the makeup of their sectors. China and Asia's ~~economy~~ economies have expanded in comparison to other less dynamic emerging market nations, prompting a swift expansion of their asset markets and a greater weight in the benchmarks. With the rising representation of Asian economies has come an increase in the weight of the financial and high-tech industries.

In the MSCI Emerging Market Index today, eight of the top ten largest individual stocks are in the consumer discretionary or information technology sectors, while one is in the finance sector. The market value of these equities is around $1.8 trillion. These top ten stocks (which make up 26% of the index) more closely replicate the NASDAQ composition than the "old" emerging market index, which was more strongly weighted toward commodities, materials, and other cyclicals.

It is assumed that emerging markets are dominated by agriculture and commodities because of a condition that existed thirty years ago. Up from 5.5% in 1997, information technology currently makes up 21% of the index. During this time, the weights of consumer discretionary, health, and real estate all increased while the weights of consumer staples and utilities decreased. In the 2000s, the weight of the energy sector rose, but in 2022, after Russian oil and gas companies were removed from the index as a result of international sanctions, that weight sharply fell. Many other sizable energy corporations in developing nations are still state-owned and not publicly traded.

Because of their new sector structure, emerging market benchmarks are now more prepared for a rising cycle than in the past. Technology companies are distinct examples of high-growth industries that depend less on the macroeconomic cycle. The performance of these companies should improve as the cycle progresses and growth becomes more limited. Banks benefit from higher rates if the yield curve does not remain inverted for an extended period. Technology and financials make up about half of the MSCI EM index; if we include consumer discretionary, these sectors make up approximately ~~two~~ two-thirds of the index (mostly e-retailing. e.g., Alibaba). For ~~low~~ low-valuation, ~~high~~ high-dividend companies that are more subject to changes in the rate of interest around the world, the Industrial and Utilities sectors presently have a combined weight of less than 10%.

Present State of Emerging Markets

- Eighty percent of benchmarks for emerging markets now consider a nation's exposure to Chinese and Asian markets. The index is more resilient to the current hiking cycle since Asia has healthier balance sheets than the typical EM countries and less severe macroeconomic imbalances.
- The weighted average ratio of foreign exchange reserves to government external debt for the MSCI Emerging Markets Index climbed from 221% in 2001 to 378% in 2017. This is partly due to the national composition and partly to the result of reserve building by most EM countries over time.
- This concentration in Asia decreases the benefits of diversification and creates additional idiosyncratic hazards. China's recent market stress is an illustration of this.
- Due to increased exposure to financial and information technology sectors—which itself is the result of increased exposure to Asia—EM equities markets are better positioned to handle

rising interest rates than in previous hiking cycles.

- Greater exposure to financials could help emerging market equity markets over developed market equity markets, but these advantages are constrained by a lower exposure to healthcare, a sector that might perform well in a rising cycle.
- EM stocks are probably going to perform more like their developed market counterparts. Greater than average historical valuation discounts relative to developed markets are one factor that may contribute to the success of EM stocks.

Conclusion

As we enter the current cycle of global tightening and rate increases, risk assets are likely to perform worse than they did during the prior periods of liquidity growth and nearly free money. The size of the market, the stability of the macroeconomy, and the industrial structure of developing countries have changed significantly over the past 20 years, though, and this suggests that they are now more prepared than in the past to deal with rising global interest rates.

EM debt has increased over the past 20 years in both foreign and local currency terms. The proportion of corporate debt to GDP has almost doubled between 2000 and 2022. The market segment may get stressful as global rates rise. Due to the fact that foreign exchange reserves have grown more swiftly than government debt denominated in hard currency, the weighted-average EMBI government is now a net creditor. Large EM countries experiencing a hard currency sovereign debt crisis are thus less likely than in the past.

The most important development in the equity markets is the domination of China, India, and the rest of Asia, which together make up almost 80% of equities market value. Compared to other EM regions, Asian economies exhibit stronger intrinsic growth drivers, larger FX reserve buffers, and fewer macroeconomic fragilities. On a sectoral level, emerging markets have shifted their attention away from banks and information technology and toward commodities, utilities, and minerals. The new sector and nation components of this asset class also suggest that EM might fare better than in previous down liquidity cycles.

Finally, compared to the inflationary cycles of the 1980s, 1990s, and 2000s, EM currencies are supported by higher real interest rates and larger foreign exchange reserves. While policy rates in some places, such as Eastern Europe, have lagged behind inflation, central banks in other regions, such as Latin America, have raised rates for a longer length of time than the Fed.

CHAPTER 4: REDUCE POVERTY THROUGH SUCCESS IN TECHNOLOGY

Despite the growth of the communication sector over the years, half of the global population still lacks a decent internet connection. After all, it is the age of the internet, and having it is an essential human right in this day and age. So, its dearth is a source of concern since a massive part of the global population has little to no access to it.

The challenge of internet unavailability is primarily a complex issue with layered solutions. First things first, it is not always a case of affordability. Other challenges also play into this lack of access.

Communication is essential for coordination and is difficult to achieve over long distances without seamless connectivity. In other words, the internet is the medium that connects anyone and everyone, regardless of distance. This seamless connectivity can move mountains on many levels. Some of them are listed below:

- Handy information mediums and services like online banking, health, education, insurance, and entertainment

- Person-to-person communication keeps friends, families, and colleagues connected.
- Seamless and ready access to resources such as goods and markets, which facilitate business and trading, ensuring increased economic prosperity and cash flow.

Second, it empowers women in society and helps them become contributing members of it. For instance, they can work from home and have greater access to services and goods from home.

Therefore, it is imperative that the entire world's population have these same economic benefits and technological conveniences that are available to half of the world. Being online can work wonders for them.

Economic Perks of the Internet

A population without internet services misses out on a variety of benefits that the internet provides and promises. It can put them at a distinct disadvantage in the following areas:

- No access to online banking
- No access to health services
- No access to educational opportunities
- No access to education
- No access to government services
- No access to consumer markets
- No way to communicate with specific relatives.

Other means of gaining access to these services can be time-consuming, often leaving only a select few options. So, a lack of internet can negatively impact the population by restricting their options to earn a living, raise their income, or improve their living standards. As a result, the bridge of opportunity grows wider and wider.

The repercussions of this exclusion are more or less similar, even though the reasons behind the exclusion are not always the same among developed and developing economies.

Furthermore, widespread access to the internet may help empower women in several regions and their societies. For example, women in undeveloped societies can take an active part in the economic growth of the country. Research also supports this. Many studies over the years have shown that increased access to mobile broadband has resulted in a significant impact on the GDP and improved people's lives. One study from the Imperial College Business School in London shows that broadband penetration can lead to a 0.6 percent to 2.8 percent rise in GDP.

Technology Means Job Creation

The demand for resources will certainly spike as the global population increases year over year. In doing so, the availability of resources available to fulfill this need will experience a shortfall. For instance, the unemployment rate continues to soar. This rate of unemployment has seen a steady rise over the years. Due to this reason, the youth have foreseen a need to acquire digital skills to earn a living since the labor market is either cutthroat or saturated. Therefore, entering this labor market has been more difficult than a few decades ago.

The recent pandemic showcased this trend, as a vast majority of people acquired digital skills. They learned and honed these skills at home, either on their phones or computers. People capitalizing on technology entered a new untapped market during the pandemic as the demand for digital services ramped up way more than before.

Digital services are here to stay.

The world has been thoroughly transformed by digital technology, raising the need for digital services as well. People rarely go a day without using a digital service. So, this has opened a new section of the job market and created new opportunities for people.

The evolution of technology enables new job openings that were previously unheard of. However, they are very much a part of society now. Many skilled professionals are employed in sectors that were nonexistent two decades ago. The following are some of the most recent new industries to emerge:

- YouTube content creators
- Data scientists
- Social media managers
- SEO experts
- Software engineers
- Software and app developers
- UX developers
- Cloud specialists

- Drone operators

The advent of technology has allowed for new job openings that did not exist a few decades ago.

On the other hand, technology has also closed the door to many skills and occupations that existed before its inception. It has disrupted work and reshaped the workspace. However, technology has introduced more jobs than it has replaced, and the ease of accessibility is even greater than before.

So, developing and developed nations that are enthusiastic about tech investment will inevitably have a continuously thriving job market. For instance, the number of software developers and programmers in the UK alone has undergone a major spike. It is living proof that technology has vastly helped economies, the job market, and economic growth in tandem. And in recent times, the demand for digital skills has only gone up in the labor market, creating new positions for job hunters in the country.

Secondly, the employment ratio can become even better when industries and governments make sound investments in ways to maximize technology. This will help businesses drum up their competency levels as they attempt to take on the big players in the industry with tech-savvy tools.

More so, the advent of machines has facilitated the existing workforce even further. They are now more productive than previously. Machines complement human labor, raise their output further, and improve the relationship between consumers and services rendered.

Needless to say, the unemployment rate has fallen significantly in recent years as the internet and digitalization have created a vast field of untapped opportunities.

Technology and Innovation Can Eradicate Poverty

History has shown that technology is a powerful instrument since it drives economic and social development. So, it should come as no surprise that it has played a monumental role in poverty reduction for vast swathes of the population in the past. As a result, it can also play a similar role in modern societies.

Technology can be deployed to wage a continuous war against poverty across the global landscape. It has a multi-dimensional application, extending its benefits in the following areas:

- Raising the agricultural production volume
- Generation of low-cost energy
- Clean water for better health outcomes

The last few decades have seen a technological explosion. The digitalization of these existing global industries and services raises the levels of prosperity, which brings about growth in many socioeconomic indicators. For instance, people now live longer on average and have healthier lives than their ancestors. Take the instance of the Industrial Revolution of the 18th century, which greatly eradicated poverty in Western Europe and European landscapes. It was the impetus that lifted people out of poverty and raised their standard of living.

Technology is both a great leapfrog and a great equalizer on its own. Its lack of access results in inequality. If, for example, digital services are extended to poor and underprivileged areas, then they can grow at a tremendous rate.

As a whole, Information and Communication Technology (ICT) can tackle the issue of poverty by disseminating access to financial, health, and educational services. As a matter of fact, even simplistic tech can vastly impact poverty reduction. The use of cell phones in Africa is a noteworthy instance of that. Similarly, new technologies vastly improve the overall outcomes for small and medium enterprises.

China is one example of a country that has made remarkable progress due to technological invasion.

The struggling nations globally are a function of bad policy, which leads to immense poverty in those settings. So, good government investment and intervention can assist in alleviating these poverty levels significantly.

Again, China is a prime example of eradicating poverty through infrastructure deployment across its landscape. That is why investing is central to eradicating poverty and propelling economic growth. Investment works differently for developed and developing economies. For instance, the richer nations often have free access to capital markets at low-interest rates, whereas the poorer countries bear a scary risk with this capital or do not have access at all. The Belt and Road Initiative (BRI) is a project that makes an offer to developing nations to collaborate for economic good by strengthening the infrastructure in key areas. These collaborative measures will put the depressed nations in a better position to shore up their economies and take a step in the right direction.

Another instance of technology driving growth is the usage of agricultural drones in China, which have become popular in China recently. These drones are common in Chinese farms, where drones spray more pesticides and fertilizers on farmland per day by drone than by humans hand. Thus, it should come as no surprise that the sales of agricultural drones skyrocketed in China just recently, driving efficiency across the board. Needless to say, this disruptive technology can spawn a new generation of more efficient, productive, and immensely profitable farms. Thanks to the advent of automation in farming, a farmer can easily manage much bigger farms, so their net income will astronomically increase.

Secondly, as mentioned earlier, mobile technology has immense potential to raise the income levels of small-scale farmers and aspiring entrepreneurs. And that is because they enjoy the same advantages of tapping into better markets. The mobile supply chain can connect the platforms and help these individuals and entities do business with thousands of others in the field, spanning a massive area. They can share ideas and suggestions on improving systems and their improvements. More so, they can also make use of the updated pricing information, which can assist in selling their produce at market-competitive rates, thus improving their socioeconomic outcomes. It is a step in the right direction.

Conclusion

Poverty is a grave and concerning challenge mostly faced by the developing world. It requires sustained and focused action ~~to reduce it significantly, break the poverty cycle, and raise~~on reducing it significantly, breaking the poverty cycle and raising the existing living standards.

Income is often deemed the yardstick for poverty measurement. However, it is not the correct measure since the concept is multidimensional and involves several aspects. It also includes aspects of sanitation, water, food, education, health, shelter, human rights, and access to important services.

The World Bank notes that the poverty index in Latin America, South Asia, and sub-Saharan Africa is the highest. The negative outcomes are consistently on the rise, thanks to modest economic performance and heightened population growth.

The arrival of technology in these depressed economies can bring about viable outcomes. Technology as a tool is powerful and can improve lives in developing countries. However, the failure of these projects in such landscapes is also common and stems from a lack of understanding regarding the local markets and personalized demands. This can be resolved in three potential ways. Firstly, concrete targets for inclusivity must be set up, and indicators to measure them are equally important. For instance, the scale and scope of the project's implementation could provide a direction for concrete measurement.

Secondly, understanding and working with the local ecosystem is just as important. This implies working with local partners within a local ecosystem. Establishing local capacity is critical to ensuring that the technology will be in use when the program concludes.

Thirdly, working with the end users during the design phase ensures the successful implementation of the program. The biggest failures in these cases involve incorporating technology, which usually brings tech that does not fully meet the needs and demands of the end users. Thus, engagement of the local communities during the testing, piloting, and unveiling of new tech solutions

These measures require important prior planning and implementation to bring struggling economies up to speed.

CHAPTER 5 – IMPROVE THE FOOD SUPPLY CHAIN

In the face of a growing global population, the need to reinvent farming systems serves as a light of progress toward relieving poverty and providing food security for all. As the number of people on our planet increases, so does the demand for food. In this setting, agricultural practices transformation takes center stage, providing a critical solution to the pressing challenge of producing food in more significant quantities and with greater efficiency.

Traditional farming methods frequently fall short of meeting the demands of a modern, interconnected society. The extension of cultivatable land is hampered by several problems, including urbanization, environmental degradation, and a scarcity of fertile soil. This requires a complete transformation that embraces innovation, research, and technology to maximize every aspect of the farming process.

Furthermore, the growth of agrotechnology provides more than enough instruments that promise to transform the farming landscape. From genetically engineered crops with increased resilience to pests and diseases to vertical farming methods that overcome traditional geographical constraints, the possible boundaries are fast growing. When implemented with care and attention, these advances have the potential to unlock previously inconceivable yields and support worldwide sustainable food production.

It is critical to remember that the goal of higher agricultural yields is about more than just numbers; it is also about quality. Farmers who use innovative approaches can grow nutrient-rich foods that alleviate malnutrition and improve general health. We can battle the cruel cycle of poverty and malnutrition by prioritizing diverse and nutritious plant kinds, ensuring that people have access to nourishment and the critical nutrients that allow them to thrive.

Policymakers play a critical role in achieving this goal. They must promote an enabling environment that encourages research and development, incentivizes sustainable practices, and enables small farmers to access the information and resources needed for significant transformation. These small farmers represent the backbone of food production in many regions.

Food is undoubtedly the most essential element of life. It is critical for our survival. Therefore, we must work together to improve and expand our food supply chain to help those living below the poverty line. There are places in this world where people cannot afford a single meal for their family. People are dying of hunger because the global food supply chain is unable to meet global food needs. Therefore, it is essential to discuss this critical issue to understand how we can protect and improve the food supply chain to achieve global prosperity.

Importance of Soil

The condition of our soil and the availability of agricultural lands are critical elements in the agricultural industry. In fact, they are the primary elements, and without them, not a gram of agricultural yield is possible. As we address the pressing issues of poverty and hunger, adequate protection of these natural resources emerges as a critical component in pursuing a sustainable, abundant food supply.

The soil is a complex and dynamic ecosystem that exists beneath the land's surface. This living medium, which is frequently overlooked, plays a significant role in deciding the success of our agricultural operations. Improving soil health is not optional; it is required to increase crop yields, increase nutrient density, and reduce food production's environmental impact.

Regenerative agricultural practices should be adopted to ensure proper soil management. Cover cropping, crop rotation, and decreased tillage are examples of regenerative agricultural practices. These approaches encourage nutrient cycling, water retention, and insect management by boosting biodiversity within the soil microbiome while strengthening the soil's resilience against deterioration. As a result, there is a harmonious balance between nature and cultivation, generating increased yields and ensuring the land's long-term survival.

Besides regenerative agricultural practices, the well-calculated application of organic matter and biofertilizers can revitalize soil fertility. This planned focus on soil health results in crops thriving in nutrient-rich environments, resulting in improved food quality and nutritional benefits for producers and consumers.

Expansion of Agricultural Lands

While maintaining the soil is critical, the limited availability of cultivatable land necessitates the development of new agricultural practices. This requirement is heightened by urbanization, climate change, and land degradation, all of which put further strain on available space. A multi-directional solution based on technology, policy, and sustainable land management is required to address these issues.

Agricultural production in urban surroundings and unused spaces is possible through vertical and rooftop farming, hydroponics, and aquaponics. These solutions provide innovative agricultural solutions for the urban population. These strategies not only maximize land efficiency but also cut transportation costs and the carbon footprint of food distribution.

Precision land management using Geographic Information Systems (GIS) and satellite imagery can aid in identifying underutilized or degraded lands that can be restored to productive use in rural areas. Land tenure and property rights are also crucial in stimulating long-term investments in soil restoration and agricultural output.

Policy measures prioritizing land conservation, reforestation, and agroforestry can help expand agricultural areas while reducing environmental deterioration. We may develop a future where rich harvests are farmed in a way that respects our planet's fragile balance by creating a healthy coexistence between agriculture and natural ecosystems.

Improving soil health and expanding agricultural lands is not the duty of a single entity; instead, these goals can be achieved through a collaborative effort between governments, farmers, researchers, and communities. The birth of a new era in food production necessitates investments in research, education, and infrastructure that will enable individuals and nations to embrace sustainable practices. In doing so, we ensure a future of plentiful harvests and improved livelihoods and create the framework for a more resilient and equitable world.

Role of Global Giants and Develop Countries

The inequalities between nations in the intricate web of global food production can be stark. Some countries enjoy technical achievements and abundant resources. In contrast, others face challenges that limit their agricultural potential. Within this divide, a powerful need emerges—the responsibility of global giants and developed nations to assist agro-based underdeveloped countries. We can positively change the global food supply chain if developed nations start sharing their agro-based knowledge and resources with developing nations.

The concept of collective progress is central to the idea of international development. Recognizing that the issues confronting agro-based developing nations are frequently worsened by limited resources, inadequate infrastructure, and technological limitations, it is evident that collaboration is critical. Global giants and wealthy countries have an abundance of expertise, research, and technologies that can be used to bridge gaps and empower nations to realize their agricultural potential.

The exchange of knowledge and expertise is at the heart of this collaboration. Developed countries can provide developing countries access to advanced research, best practices, and training programs encouraging local farmers to adopt modern and sustainable farming techniques. Workshops, exchange programs, and technology transfer initiatives can help spread innovative approaches ranging from precision agriculture to integrated pest control, allowing local farmers to maximize yields while mitigating risks.

Moreover, infrastructure development is critical to agricultural advancement. Global stakeholders and rich nations can play a crucial role by investing in critical infrastructure, including irrigation systems, storage facilities, and transportation networks. These enhancements not only increase the overall efficiency of the value chain but also offer agro-based nations the tools they need to maximize crop production and decrease post-harvest losses.

In addition, access to resources is a critical component of agricultural development. Collaborative initiatives can include distributing better seeds, fertilizers, and equipment customized to the unique demands of local ecosystems. We can build the groundwork for increased yields and greater resilience in the face of environmental problems by ensuring farmers have access to high-quality inputs.

Furthermore, developed countries can aid the agro-based developing nations in developing and implementing efficient agricultural policies, as well as building local institutions, which can provide an enabling environment for sustainable farming practices. Moreover, campaigning for fair trade and equitable market access ensures that increasing crop yields translate into better livelihoods and economic progress.

Global giants and developed nations must embrace the collaborative approach to make this world a just and equitable society. This is probably the only way to eradicate poverty and increase the global food supply chain.

Importance of Fertilizer

Few factors have as much sway in the complicated mechanism of agricultural productivity as the availability and application of proper fertilizers. Fertilizers are the bloodline of crops, ensuring the transportation of nutrients and protecting them from pests. A good fertilizer is as essential for an excellent yield as oxygen for survival.

Fertilizers have sparked an agricultural revolution by delivering vital nutrients that promote plant growth, resulting in higher yields and healthier crops. The availability of balanced nutrients like nitrogen, phosphorus, and potassium is critical for developing strong plants that can fight pests, diseases, and environmental challenges. However, the transforming power of fertilizers is only completely realized when they are of good quality and used correctly.

Access to high-quality fertilizers is not merely a matter of convenience; it is essential for small farmers and agro-based communities seeking to increase agricultural productivity. Substandard or counterfeit fertilizers can undermine efforts, resulting in lower yields, soil deterioration, and eventually perpetuating poverty cycles.

Efforts to ensure the availability of high-quality fertilizers cover a wide range of activities. In partnership with international organizations and the private sector, governments play a critical role in defining fertilizer production and distribution norms and standards. Quality control procedures, certification processes, and public awareness campaigns can all help to create an ecology in which farmers can buy fertilizers with confidence that they will provide the desired results.

Sustainable farming techniques require effective fertilizer use. It is not just about giving nutrients to the soil but also about maintaining balance. Fertilizer overuse can result in nutrient runoff, water pollution, and ecological imbalances. Precision agricultural techniques, soil testing, and agronomic advisory enable farmers to customize fertilizer delivery to individual crop and soil demands. We can protect the environment while reaping the benefits of increased harvests by optimizing fertilizer consumption.

Access to quality fertilizers can be transformative for smallholder farmers, who make up a significant share of worldwide agricultural labor. Agricultural extension services, farmer cooperatives, and community-based initiatives can give these farmers the information and tools they need to make informed fertilizer selection, application, and management decisions. It is necessary to assist these farmers to break the cycle of subsistence and embark on a path of success by providing them with tools to enhance their harvests.

The importance of excellent fertilizers in pursuing higher crop yields cannot be neglected. We can construct a future where access to these important resources is universal, and farmers are empowered to cultivate plenty that reaches far beyond their fields through collaboration, creativity, and devotion. We can cultivate the seeds of wealth and growth by investing in the sustenance of the land, fostering a world where the promise of a bountiful harvest is within reach of all.

Conclusion

A strong and efficient food supply chain is vital for global prosperity. The food supply chain, at its core, is a driver of economic empowerment. It comprises various operations, from agricultural production and processing to distribution and retail, contributing to job creation, investment stimulation, and economic expansion. Millions of people rely on it for a living, from smallholder farmers tending to their fields to entrepreneurs innovating in the agribusiness industry. As the food supply chain grows, so do local and global economies, creating a path to wealth that crosses boundaries.

Moreover, the food supply chain's interconnection creates openings for international trade and market access. It acts as a channel for surplus production to reach areas of lack, facilitating a worldwide interchange of products and resources. This interaction improves food security and fosters economic resilience by diversifying revenue streams and opening doors for international collaboration. Furthermore, as developing countries improve their capacities in the food supply chain, they are better positioned to compete in the global economy, resulting in increasing foreign exchange profits and decreased reliance.

In addition, the food supply chain serves as a breeding ground for technical advancement and innovation. From precision agriculture to smart logistics, the sector constantly evolves technologically. These advances boost productivity and resource efficiency and encourage the development of new sectors and job possibilities.

Moreover, the food supply chain promotes social cohesion by addressing basic necessities. Access to nutritious food promotes healthy populations, lowering illness burdens and boosting overall quality of life. Furthermore, as communities develop due to agricultural operations, social structures are strengthened, cultural identities are recognized, and individuals enjoy a sense of purpose and dignity. This connectivity between the food supply system and societal well-being generates a tapestry that promotes a flourishing global human experience.

When we consider the importance of the food supply chain to global prosperity, we are reminded of its far-reaching implications. We can sow the seeds of development, cultivate the landscapes of opportunity, and reap a harvest of global prosperity by investing in the improvement of the food supply chain.

CHAPTER 6: DATA-DRIVEN ECONOMIES

What is economy?

There are different ways to define the economy. In simpler terms, an economy is the system that manages the goods and services in a region. It includes the manufacturing, distribution, and consumption of products.

Another definition that further explains this multifaceted system is that an economy is formed when people with different skills, interests, and goals come together to be better off and trade with others.

An economy is commonly used as a measuring tool that describes how resources can be used effectively and how products can be produced and consumed.

In a broader sense, an economy works by establishing a complex network of relevant resource and product markets and businesses along with their potential traders. These markets distribute resources that are limited among the candidates within that market. This man-made system is modified to fulfill the needs of a population.

An economy can be divided into three types, considering their significant characteristics. These include capitalist economy, mixed economy, and socialist economy. These three types are based on the extent of a trader's liberty and profit motive.

Two important economic factors that help us to measure accurately how well or badly an economy performs include microeconomics and macroeconomics. A global organization, the International Monetary Fund (IMF), refers to macroeconomics as the aspect of the economy that focuses on the performance of a prevalent economy of a country as a whole, such as gross domestic product (GDP), unemployment rates, and inflation. On the other hand, microeconomics studies the behavior of a household or businesses regarding the utilization and allocation of resources, such as the supply and demand of goods and services.

What benefits do data-driven economies offer?

We need to understand what ~~does~~ "Data-Driven Economies" exactly mean before exploring its advantages. Data-driven economies focus on data rather than mere intuition when decisions are being made. This contemporary approach offers measurable benefits because of the fact that this economic strategy uses facts and figures instead of gut instinct.

This economic system centers its attention on data or hard information to drive innovation, efficiency, and growth in a region. This advanced approach proved to be transformative as it grants new shape to the system of production, consumption, and allocation of goods and services.

Data analytics is involved whenever the analysis of a large data is concerned. It is necessary to extract relevant and useful information from the bulk of data.

Cutting-edge technologies such as Quantum Computing, Artificial Intelligence (AI), Machine Learning (ML), and more enable organizations to identify and process patterns, correlations, and fluctuating trends within large volumes of datasets.

In today's world, ranging from big industries like healthcare to small-scale industries like toy manufacturing have embraced data-driven approaches.

In hospitals, data mining of patients can be helpful in personalized treatments. Accounting firms use data to predict possible credit risks and fraudulent activities. Agricultural industries can transform farming techniques to optimize irrigation, planting, and harvesting by following data analysis skills. Data search and content analytics help manufacturing industries further enhance the performance of the production process and supply chain.

Giant Tech Companies like Microsoft, Amazon, and Google have leveraged data and introduced new business models. Their personalized services and targeted advertisement not only optimized their overall performance but provided valuable insights into customer behavior, market trends, and more. This economic strategy helped them to gain a competitive advantage in the market.

Data-driven economies involve not only numbers but also foster greater confidence in business decisions. Governments can get clarity on opportunities, can predict more accurately, can improve agility, and have the ability to expand scale. This approach leads to incredible benefits if we adopt it to boost our economy.

This chapter will shed light on different areas related to data-driven economies. Methods that provide measurable results of economic policies will be discussed in detail. We get to know how we can make decisions more efficient, why it is necessary to employ data analysis when decisions are being made, and how we can improve the efficiency of our economy. What steps should we take to ensure a better economy?

How ~~to~~ do we come up with methods that provide measurable results of economic policies?

International Organizations such as the Bureau of Labor Statistics (BLS) and the Organization for Economic Co-operation and Development (OECD) work to monitor economic growth. Statisticians use several methods to track economic progress.

Methods that involve a systematic approach can be developed to achieve measurable outcomes of economic policies. These include setting clear objectives, collecting comprehensive data, analyzing it rigorously, and interpreting it accurately.

It is of profound importance to introduce and design such methods that effectively yield measurable consequences of economic policies. Economists and policymakers can be aware of the impacts of these economic policies and make efforts in their implementation. These steps help them assess the effectiveness and make informed and efficient decisions.

Here's a comprehensive guide on how to develop methods that provide measurable results of economic policies:

Start with clear definitions of your objectives. Evaluate the economic policies you would like to modify. Primarily focus on boosting GDP as it is the fundamental measure of evaluation of economic performance. Other objectives may include bringing the unemployment rate down significantly and addressing salary inequality. Objectives with better outlines form a strong base to measure impact.

Selecting those indicators that align with the aims of policies helps you in tracking performance. Indicators refer to the variables that indicate changes you wish to bring. To understand this, let's take an example of employment. If your policy aims to improve it, indicators like labor force participation and job creation opportunities might be considered.

It is important to collect relevant baseline data before implementing the policy. Be careful~~, t~~. This data should be relevant, accurate, and consistent because it will serve as a major point of reference when we measure the impact of our newly amended policies.

After the collection of data, the next step should be its interpretation and implementation. Changes can be brought about by taxation, expenditures, government regulation affairs, or any other measures.

Regular collection of data before, during, or after the implementation of policy allows you to track and closely monitor changes over time. Apply suitable statistical analysis to analyze the data. It may include difference-in-differences analysis, regression analysis, or other econometric techniques.

By establishing comparisons and causalities, you can measure the influence of the policies on the ground. Other methods may include surveys, case studies, and interviews. In this way, you can better understand the overall effectiveness of the policy.

Efficient decision-making can only be done with data at our disposal. Data analysis should be made necessary to ensure effective decision-making.

Efficient decision-making is the process that allows you to make informed choices. This effective step-by-step process helps you to identify a desired decision, collect and organize relevant information, and find alternative resolutions.

This area relies heavily on making decision-making efficient. As the data is the cornerstone of this process, we need to understand it to solve complexities, predict outcomes, and evaluate alternatives. Making deliberate and thoughtful decisions paves the way to the achievement of the goal. And to achieve it, we need relevant and accurate data at our disposal.

There are many reasons. Let's find out why data is necessary to make efficient decisions.

Data-driven decisions are free of personal biases and judgments. Data helps you to view situations neutrally and make decisions based on factual information rather than gut feelings. It provides context to decisions. You need to consider historical trends and then the current situation. This contextual understanding also facilitates you to gain insight into potential future scenarios.

Assessment of available Information empowers you to come up with efficient strategies and policies. You can anticipate future results with certainty with the help of trends and patterns that data displayed.

Complex problems can be broken down into more manageable components if you employ a systematic and structured approach. Data is crucial as it serves as the foundation for objective and evidence-based decisions. Therefore, efficient decision-making hinges strongly on the provided information.

Data analysis is equally of great importance as data collection. Data analysis refers to the process of examining and interpreting data. It assists you to identify and extract meaningful information. It can be in the form of trends and patterns.

Data analysis is a vital tool to move along with our complex and rapidly evolving world. It improves our quality of making thoughtful decisions in various domains.

There are several reasons that answer the question of why data analysis is a prerequisite for effective decision-making.

Data analysis facilitates you to make decisions based on facts instead of assumptions and groundless speculations. It helps us to defend our decisions by relying on empirical evidence and saves us from making biased and irrational decisions.

Sometimes, we need to consider multiple variables to address certain decisions. By analyzing data carefully, we can put forward more organized solutions.

Strategic planning can only be done after gathering data from reliable sources and analysis of its key points. Market trends, competitive landscape, and other critical factors assist you better in choosing your informed strategic direction.

Risk management is also a crucial factor that informs you regarding the risks associated with different choices. Data analysis enables you to take proactive steps in order to manage and mitigate these threatening risks effectively.

Another remarkable aspect that data analysis offers is the continuous improvements. You can refine strategies and adjust approaches after analyzing the consequences.

In a data-rich era, effective decision-making demands a powerful emphasis on data analysis strategies. Ultimately, it is high time to use data analysis skills to attain optimal outcomes in a tangled and interconnected world.

How to improve economic efficiency?

We discussed the effective methods that are certainly helpful in achieving desired results in response to implementing economic policies in detail. Then, we were informed about the major role of data analysis in the optimization of decision-making. Now, this area will cover the steps that can be taken to boost the efficiency of the economy.

Economic efficiency can be defined in simple words as maximum benefit and low manufacturing cost. It presents a balance between profit and loss. It is an economic condition where resources are distributed optimally with minimum wastage.

To improve economic efficiency is the primary goal of governments, businesses, and communities as a whole. It can only be achieved when resources are utilized appropriately.

Here's a guide on how to further enhance the level of production, distribution, and consumption of goods and ultimately improve economic efficiency.

Compel businesses to bring new ideas to the table to address the reduction of production costs and ameliorate quality. To ensure fair competition, design such regulatory frameworks that promote efficiency.

It is not possible to make your economy efficient and competitive without conducting proper research. It is substantial to invest in Research and Development (R&D) to survive in this highly technological era. Employ rising technologies such as the Internet of Things (IoT), automation, and artificial intelligence (AI) to advance in technology.

Resources must be allocated efficiently. Pricing mechanisms must be reviewed and amended to ensure efficient use of resources and encourage minimizing waste.

Governments and businesses must consider cost-benefit ~~analyzes~~ analyses before making a decision. This approach will definitely result in the highest net benefits.

Bringing improvements to the economy is a continuous process that requires contemporary solutions. It is the utmost duty of governments and businesses to establish an environment that fosters collaboration and competition.

Conclusion

We've learned that we all play a part in building and stability of the economy because it affects us in several ways. We have to consider the possible factors to better contribute toward it as it is all around us. The economy outlined our living standards, employment rates, government expenditures, and, mainly, our quality of life.

These three detailed discussed areas highlight the importance of using data in making the economy efficient. No doubt, a data-driven economy indicates a paradigm shift and opens doors to limitless opportunities in various domains.

CHAPTER 7 – LIFT ALL SANCTIONS

This chapter unfolds the different but significant aspects of sanctions. Like the true and simple definition of sanctions, its extensive types, its vast effects, and how sanctions are hindering the nation's economic growth. This unit will also enlighten us on what we can offer as global giants to allow developing nations to grow financially and socially. How lifting sanctions can be a stimulus in the improvement of international relations between countries. Moreover, in what ways can traditional life once again reemerge as a result of the removal of economic barriers?

What Are Sanctions?

There are two contrasting meanings of the word "sanction." In simpler words, the sanction is a legal or formal approval. But it can also mean a threatened penalty to make people obey a law. This chapter deals with the latter definition of the term.

Sanctions refer to a range of penalties imposed on a country by one or more countries. Sanctions can also be applied by international organizations or alliances upon another entity or individual in case of violations of laws, agreements, or human rights. These strategies are fundamentally intended to exert pressure, induce behavioral change, or coerce a targeted party. This strain certainly leads to bring about economic, political, or diplomatic shifts. Sanctions can last for three months for the first higher-level sanction for a year and five months for every other higher-level sanction.

Sanctions can be aimed to compel or deterrence in order to achieve a desired outcome. It serves as a useful policy tool. It is generally imposed on smaller or developing countries. At the present time, there are three principal entities responsible for levying sanctions: the European Union (EU), the United Nations (UN), and the Organization for Security and Cooperation in Europe (OSCE).

The effectiveness of sanctions can be positive or negative. In the case of Iran's nuclear program, negotiations were made possible. In other instances, they may harden the resolution of penalized countries such as North Korea.

Over the past century, international use of sanctions has increased. As of 2023, Russia is the most sanctioned country in the world.

Types of Sanctions

Below are various types of sanctions to broaden your understanding.

Economic sanctions: it is the most common type of sanctions. It encompasses trade, financial transactions, and investments with the entity. It includes trade sanctions, export control, freezing of assets, and even boycotts. These steps prohibit trade between nations and limit the transfer of goods, services, or technologies. Freezing of assets prevents them from accessing their financial resources held abroad. Boycotting covers the complete ban or cessation of business ties with the sanctioned country.

Diplomatic sanctions: These are the actions taken to sever diplomatic relations between countries. Restrictions on diplomatic communications involve the closure of embassies or the recall of ambassadors.

Travel restrictions: It prevents the residents of the affected country from moving to other countries.

Military embargoes: This type of sanction restrains the country from possessing weapons or military equipment to minimize the potential for conflict.

Industrial sanctions: These sectorial sanctions aim at industries of the country to restrict its technology transfers or economy.

Smart sanctions: it is also known as targeted sanctions. It does not impose broad restrictive measures on the entire population. Rather, it basically focuses on individuals or institutions for abhorrent actions. This approach minimizes the intensity and directs only to responsible ones.

Multilateral sanctions: These involve the collective action of multiple countries or global bodies against the targeted entity. It has a tendency to have greater global authority.

Sanctions can be exacted to achieve specific political, economic, or diplomatic objectives. Potential consequences must be carefully considered while promulgating sanctions, as they will take hold of both innocent people and responsible entities.

How Sanctions Play a Role in Deteriorating the Development of the Targeted Country?

Sanctions can have the most detrimental impact on a nation's development. These effects are wide-ranging and complex. They crumble the economic, social, and political dimensions of a nation. The outcomes depend on the severity of the imposed sanctions, the resilience of the economy, and its policies.

Presently, many countries are struggling due to crippling sanctions that are hindering the nation's growth.

Some common effects are worth explaining.

Economic impact: One of the paramount effects of sanctions is to limit economic activities. Economic sanctions severely damage the economy of the country. These impacts induce economic contraction and stagnation by restricting trade, isolating finances, and limiting foreign investment. These sanctions lead to undesired consequences such as inflation and high unemployment rates. One of the leading causes is a sharp decline in revenue in the country. The resulting decay in economic growth impedes its ability to function properly.

Humanitarian outcomes: One of the most concerning effects of sanctions on developing countries is their potential to inflame humanitarian crises. Sanctions hinder the transportation of food, medicine, and medical supplies. This leads to decreased accessibility to basic life necessities and healthcare services. This hindrance poses a threat to vulnerable populations such as infants, the terminally ill, and the elderly.

Bankruptcy: One of the devastating effects of sanctions is the economic downturn. This directly contributes to poverty and unemployment. Businesses or industries may shut down because of the limited access to resources. Poorer segments of the population suffer disproportionately. This widens inequality within developing countries.

Depreciation of currency: When exports, foreign investments, and capital flight have been reduced, the currency of the country will ultimately devalue. The devaluation of currency contributes to inflation and minimizes the purchasing power of a nation. The economic hardship dwindles job opportunities and strains the social safety net without adequate support.

Impact on education: crippling sanctions undoubtedly have a detrimental influence on education and technology. This elementary aspect affects government funding for education. This will limit pollution to achieve quality schooling and hinder human capital development. Moreover, this compromise makes the approach to international markets and technologies unattainable and suffocates the country's long-term research and development advancement.

Political instability: Sanctions play a part in the erosion of democracy as it creates an environment of economic turmoil and limitless uncertainty. It results in complex political consequences in developing countries. The democratic processes and civil liberties are suppressed. This will lead to a lack of governance reform and hampered inclusive development. Social unrest may rise as the population voices frustrations over worsening living conditions.

Redirection to informal economies: Economic challenges compel individuals and businesses to informal economies or black markets. This might offer short-term relief, but on the other hand, it can lead to corruption and criminal or illegal activities. To increase access to goods and services, this shift further destabilizes the nation's formal economy.

To mitigate the vast and negative effects of the imposed sanctions, it is important for the international community to explore alternative methods of achieving policy goals that reduce harm to innocent civilians and promote a stable global landscape.

How Global Giants May Help Stumbling Economies?

Global giants must consider lifting the sanctions and allow developing nations to grow economically and socially. The world has become a global village. Therefore, the well-being of developing nations is a matter of global concern. It presents both sides of the debate. Some argue that suspension of sanctions fosters development, improves lifestyle, and a stable economy. On the contrary, opponents raise concerns about peace and security.

Global giants as influential authorities must seriously consider the situation of developing nations and ease sanctions. There are a number of compelling reasons and ways through which sanctions can be removed and let the targeted country have the opportunity to grow, develop, and prosper.

Here is a detailed section on how global giants can contribute to economic stability by lifting sanctions.

Humanitarian Imperative: sanctions not only affect the targeted population but also the innocent individuals who are at risk due to bad medical conditions. By abolishing punitive measures, global giants can contribute to improving the overall well-being and survival of civilians.

Promoting human rights: Sanctions adversely affect the basic human rights of the population at a large scale. Refinement of sanctions can improve the human rights conditions in developing nations. Governments can be able to allocate resources to education, healthcare, and social services. Respecting human rights and upholding laws facilitate an environment of dignity and equality for all.

Sustainable development: Global giants must remove trade barriers to spur economic growth, increase employment rates, and boost industrialization. It is crucial for their sustainable development.

International relations: Rebuilding diplomatic relations between nations requires the removal of sanctions. It serves as a gesture of goodwill. This will open the door for increased cooperation, dialogue, and collaboration on regional and global challenges. It will positively affect both developed and developing nations as it will maintain global peace and security in the region.

Ethical responsibility: Global giants have an ethical responsibility to reflect on the outcomes of their decisions on the global landscape. They should acknowledge the fact that citizens have no control over policies and actions that lead to sanctions. By lifting sanctions, they can show a firm commitment to the well-being of guiltless folks. Additionally, it must align with social responsibility and solidarity.

The decision for global giants to consider removing sanctions and allowing developing countries to develop lies in a commitment to human rights, economic development, global stability, and ethical responsibility. In comparison to concerns related to sanctions lifting, the potential positive outcomes are numerous.

Global giants have the power to shape a more equitable and prosperous world for all.

What Positive Effects Can Result from the Abolition of Sanctions on International Relations?

Sanctions cancelation not only improves the international relations between countries but also the traditional way of life. It plays a significant role in refining global ties and fostering a more collaborative and constructive environment.

Here's how the removal of sanctions ameliorates foreign relations and enhances regional stability.

Diplomacy: When sanctions are removed, the country will be able to engage in positive dialogue. This action demonstrates the resolution of the dispute through peaceful means and paves the way to meaningful negotiation.

Trust rebuilding: It will transmit a green signal that a country is willing to work towards common goals and discuss a wide range of issues openly.

Unrest in the region: These positive and encouraging steps ensure that the targeted country resolves any conflict or dispute peacefully without causing unrest in the region.

Economic cooperation: It will create endless opportunities for enhanced economic cooperation. They may sign trade agreements that benefit both parties. Coordination further facilitates investment partnerships and technological exchanges.

Cultural exchanges: It will foster a friendly atmosphere in the neighborhood. Abolishing sanctions helps the nations to exchange their cultures, promoting understanding and appreciation between countries. There are various mediums, such as educational programs, entertainment collaborative projects, and athletic events.

Global challenges: Collaborative efforts are crucial to address or curb global challenges like climate change, pandemics, and resource depletion. With the ease of sanctions, nations are able to create an environment where countries across the globe can cooperate to find solutions that benefit every human being.

What Role Does the Lifting of Sanctions Play in the Re-Emergence of the Traditional Way of Life?

Sanctions can have profound impacts on the traditional ways of life in the targeted countries. The elimination of sanctions alleviates the negative and bitter effects of the ban and helps in preserving and promoting traditional ways of life.

Here's how the traditional way of life will once again reemerge as a result.

Cultural preservation: Traditional ways of life often include unique cultural practices, rituals, and languages. Elimination of the ban helps the masses enjoy their way of life once again. It serves as a breathing room for economics that is required to preserve and revitalize cultural heritage.

Transmission of knowledge: Difficult economic conditions force the young generation to seek opportunities outside of the region. This free environment provides an opportunity to stay and learn from elders.

Social bonds: Freedom from these strains fosters strong social bonds within communities. It contributes to social cohesion that is necessary for maintaining traditional communities.

Economic livelihood: Our communities depend on specific economic activities such as agriculture, handmade crafts, or fishing. Sanctions disrupt these livelihoods. Therefore, the lift of the ban restores the traditional way of life and eases economic hardships. It can create opportunities for these communities to regain stability and resume their economic practices.

In conclusion, sanctions removal can lead to a more peaceful and stable world if we foster cooperation and understanding between nations.

Made in the USA
Monee, IL
04 November 2026

67376081R00046